Best
Termite Control

Cameron Eisner

Best Termite Control
by Cameron Eisner

ISBN 978-1-926917-22-1

Printed in the United States of America

Copyright © 2010 Psylon Press

All rights reserved. Except for use in a review, no portion of this book may be reproduced in any form without the express written permission of the author. For information regarding permission, write to
admin@psylonpress.com

Neither the author nor the publisher assumes any responsibility for the use or misuse of information contained in this book.

Other books by Psylon Press:

100% Blonde Jokes
R. Cristi
ISBN 978-0-9866004-1-8

Choosing a Dog Breed Guide
Eric Nolah
ISBN 978-0-9866004-5-6

Best Pictures Of Paris
Christian Radulescu
ISBN 978-0-9866004-8-7

Best Gift Ideas For Women
Taylor Timms
ISBN 978-0-9866004-4-9

Top Bikini Pictures
Taylor Timms
ISBN 978-0-9866426-3-0

Cross Tattoos
Johnny Karp
ISBN 978-0-9866426-4-7

Beautiful Breasts Pictures
Taylor Timms
ISBN 978-1-926917-01-6

For more books please visit:
www.psylonpress.com

TABLE OF CONTENTS

INTRODUCTION	5
WHAT ARE TERMITES?	9
HOW TERMITES WORK	19
TYPES OF TERMITES	27
DETECTING TERMITES	35
NATURAL TERMITE CONTROL	41
OTHER FORMS OF TERMITE CONTROL	49
PREVENTING TERMITES	63
CHOOSING AN EXTERMINATOR	71
CONCLUSION	77

INTRODUCTION

Little bugs and pest in your home can prove to be a minor annoyance. However, most insects that get into your home are fairly easy to control. If you have a fly or two, you can swat it or spray it. If you find a spider web in your home, simply kill the spider and dust away the web. Ants, while a little more problematic, are easy to control with ant bait and spray. If you have you ever had a problem with pests in your home or your business, you know that you do what you can to not only protect your family, but your home or building as well.

With that being said, you also know that some types of pests are easier to get rid of than others, but any home or business owner will tell you the one pest they fear the most is termites. Termites are nasty little pests that are not only difficult to control, but are extremely hard to detect until it is already too late.

Termites can ruin your home, make it hard to sell and can be costly to get rid of after the infestation occurs. In fact, termites are often called the "silent destroyer" and for good reason. A colony of termites that makes its way into your home and wood work can cause thousands of dollars of damage in no time at all. In addition, a lot of termites can survive in hidden places for a long time before you even know they have become a problem.

There are many different types of termites and each one will feed off a different food source, but all termites will thrive on the things most often found in and around homes—food source, dampness and moisture, shelter and optimal temperature. If you have these things, then you should learn more about termites and what they can do to affect your home. You will find that termites do not discriminate either. They can attack large buildings, small homes and any other type of building structure.

The good news is that there are many things you can do to prevent or reduce the chances of termites and there are ways to get rid of them after you are infested.

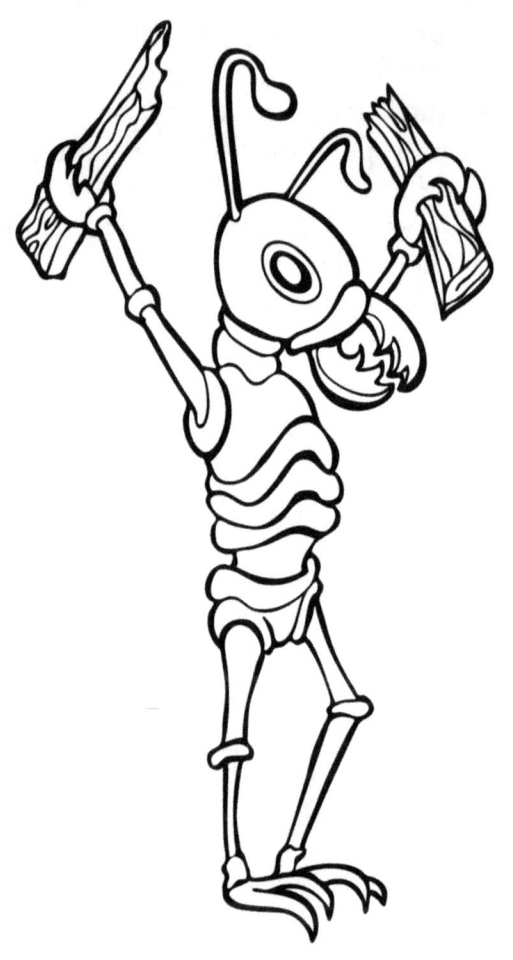

WHAT ARE TERMITES?

How much do you know about termites? If you have never been personally affected by these little insects, you may have never given them a second thought. However, if you are home owner or a business owner and care about your biggest investment, then you should learn more about termites and what you can do to prevent the destruction that they will cause.

Here is a closer look at the little insect known as the termite.

As mentioned, termites are insects that live in colonies, very similar to ants. Termites will live, work and breed together. Research has shown that in termite colonies, there are an equal number of males and females, even among the solider caste.

You might also be interested to know that there are 1900 known species of termites that live all around the world. You should also know that termites have a purpose too. While they are certainly destructive when they choose to colonize on your home, they are also very beneficial. They feed off of wood and they are the most basic type of recycling on earth.

Old insects:

Termites are not new to the earth either. Their existence can be traced back to about 350 million years and even over all of those years they have overcome climate change and other environmental changes to evolve and survive.

In addition, unlike other insects, termites have never developed a resistance to pesticides. It is believed that this is the case because the worker termites will taste and process all food sources before it is fed to the queen. This prevents the resistance that some insect develop over time. This is good information for us and it is the reason why many of the treatments that are used today are very effective in controlling and eliminating the termites that are found in and around your building structure.

The Termite Colonies:

In order to understand how termites live and breed and cause so much destruction so quickly, you must understand how the colonies work. It is quite interesting as well.

The insect:

Termites fall under the group of "eusocial" insects, and are normally classified as the taxonomic rank of order Isoptera. Termites are detritivores, meaning they feed off of dead plants, forms of wood, leaf litter, soil and animal dung.

Termites are very similar to ants, wasps and bees because they live and work together. There is a rank of labor with the queen being at the top of the rank. Also like ants, bees and wasps, termites divide the work to be done according to gender and care for the young.

With eusocial insects, the size of the colonies can range to small to huge. There are colonies that are as small as a few hundred and as big as several million. Depending on the size of the colony, there may be one queen or several. All of the queens in a colony lay eggs to help populate the colony in overlapping increments so there is always a fresh source of workers.

Termites also use a sort of "swarm" intelligence to communicate about food sources that are available. Swarm intelligence means that the termites communicate with one another about their environment. They communicate by the pheromones that their body secretes. This will help the other termites in their colony know where to go for warmth, food sources, shelter and moisture---the four things that all termite colonies must have to live and breed successfully.

Working class system:

There are many ways of eradicating termites. Many of the various forms of termite control will depend on the size of the colony. Home termite control has made huge advances once it was understood how the colonies worked as a whole. When talking about termites, you should understand that they are more than a big crowd of unwanted pests. These pests are highly advanced and organized. They have evolved over the millions of years in order to survive in today's environment. Part of the termites' success has a lot to do with their working class system.

Within a termite colony, you will find the queen (or several queens), the nymphs, workers, soldiers and the male reproductive termites, often called the king. All of these different classes of termites are vital to the success of the colony and if you eradicate one class of termites, then there is a good chance that the colony will not survive.

Colony Organization:

Termites live together, so if you find one in your home, you should know that there will be more. It is just a matter of finding their food source. You can kill off the whole colony by killing off a whole class or the whole colony. You cannot kill off a termite colony by killing only a handful of the little pests.

Take a look at how termite colonies are organized.

- *Queens:*

With ants, bees and wasps, the colonies will only have one queen. This is not always the case when it comes to termites. In many cases, especially if the termite colony is large, there could be more than one queen. The queen is the highest ranking termite in the colony.

If there is more than one queen, then there is the primary queen. This is more often than not, the first termite that founded the colony. The secondary queens, or the other queens, will also help with the egg laying duties and can take over if the primary queen dies. The queen (or queens) are waited on by the worker termites and will mate with the king.

The queen is easy to identify because she is much larger than all of the other termites. She usually has a white colored body and a small, sandy brown head. Her large body enables her to lay millions of eggs each year.

- *King:*

Even though there may be more than one queen in a colony, there is only one termite king. The king termite is the one termite who mates with the queen. The king plays an important role in the population in the colony.

He also helps in raising the younger termites while the queens lay eggs. If the king is killed, another reproductive termite will take over the reproductive duties with the queen.

The king is smaller than the queen and usually has a darker colored body with light colored wings.

- *Soldiers:*

The soldier termites also play a very important role in the success of the colony. As the name of this termite suggest, the soldier termite works to defend the colony from other insects and intruders. This termite is easy to identify when you are looking at it, no matter which species it belongs to. It has the appearance of a soldier and looks threatening. The solider termites stay very close to the nest. They also look as if they could bite or pinch. They have heads that are dark in color and rather large compared with other termites in the colony. In fact, they can be double in size. Some species can spray chemicals from their head and have large mandibles used for crushing invaders.

- *Worker Termites:*

Each type of termite is very important to the survival of the colony and the worker termite is no different. The worker termite will stay inside the colony and if you have an infestation in your home, you are not likely to see these termites. There primary responsibilities include taking care of the eggs and the larva and gathering food from the food source.

The worker termites are rather small, and light colored. They have a very soft body. If they venture outside the colony's shelter, they can die rather quickly due to sunlight exposure. If you see something that resembles a small white ant, then you are probably looking at a worker termite outside of the colony. These termites are almost always blind and susceptible to death by excessive heat.

Worker termites make up the majority of the colony population and are extremely important to the colony. In addition to caring for the eggs and gathering food, they can also help maintain and build tunnels and help with grooming of other caste members.

- *Reproductive Members:*

There is another class of termites within the mound. These are the reproductive members, also commonly known as the neotenics or the swarmers. If you see winged termites, then these are the ones you are looking at.

The reproductive members are the ones that are commonly seen outside the colonies and will fly around in groups or in swarms as they attempt to start a new nest or colony. Any reproductive member has the potential to become a queen, either of the existing colony if the queen dies or is killed or if she starts a new nest. In addition, the queen is not the mother of all the termites in the colony. The reproducers take part in this as well.

The winged reproductives will fly for short periods of time and once a new nest or home is found, she will shed her wings and begin reproducing.

Within the colony, these termites will produce the offspring in the colony and will swarm at certain times of the year. The weather and environmental conditions will often dictate when these termites swarm. If conditions for a colony become unfavorable, they will swarm then as well.

HOW TERMITES WORK

Termites are very similar to ants, wasps and bees because they live and work together. Now that you know more about termites and how they work together within the colony, you may wonder how they work together to attack your home and what you can do to prevent these pests from wreaking havoc on your building structure.

There are many different species of termites (which will be discussed more later). When you find that you are affected by termites, the way that seek out the best termite control products is to determine how the colony came to be, the size and the type of termites. Pest and termite control products will work only if you are using them on the corresponding termite colony that you have.

So, how do termites work? How do they choose your home over another? The answer many times has to do with the type of termites in your area and if you are unwittingly providing just the right mixture of things they need to survive.

- **Starting a colony:**

    Termites will start a colony when the conditions are optimal for their survival. But, where they end up living has a lot to do with what species of termites they are. Each species of termites live differently and they feed off of different food sources and materials. Some types of termites need wood to survive and these are the ones that as a homeowner will cause you the most problems if they invade your home.

There are also species of termites that do not live off of wood. They live in mounds that they build in the ground. Some types of termites live in trees, dead wood, on the outside of trees in a nest they have built or even underground. It is also very common to find some types of termites that live on poles and wooden fences. There are also termites that can cause damage to your home if they are subterranean termites. They may build a nest near your home, but feed of the wood. These can cause just as much damage as the ones that nest in your home.

- **Types of termite homes:**

There are different ways that termites live and if your home is near a location that is ideal for a certain type of termite, you may find different types of infestations. Termites don't just tunnel in the wood of your home. As mentioned above, they can also build underground tunnels, build nests and in trees.

Termites that build nests can actually build very large nests that are very easy to see. They have the ability to build very large structures by using a variety of materials found in nature. These most commonly include mud, chewed wood, soil, animal dung and saliva.

Not only will the termite nest serve as a shelter, but they are also built to collect water and provide reproductive chambers to ensure the colony population. These nests are quite advanced because they have tunnels that provide for a good balance of air and temperature. The tunnels also help the termites travel through the nest efficiently.

It is common to see large termite nests built on pieces of timber and fallen trees. If you find a large nest near your home, it is not recommended that you try a do it yourself termite control. You will need to call a professional to help you remove these pests from your property.

Termite mounds are just as advanced and well made as large nests. These are most commonly seen in Africa and Australia where they are known as "anthills", although they are not really ant hills at all. These above ground nests can be very large and can house thousands of termites. In fact, some of the largest above ground mounds have been about 27 feet tall, although the typical size is much smaller.

The shape of these types of termite mounds can vary as much as the size of the mound itself. Some of them are shaped as domes, while others have tall looking towers or cone shape.

Many times, these types of termite mounds are covered in organic material such as weeds, grass, shrubs and mud. In some areas where these mounds are common, they dominate the landscape. There is a purpose for the shape of these types of termite mounds. The tall cone shaped mounds serve as a way for the inside of the mound to get proper circulation and air. The inside of the mound often features a fungal garden that many species of termites keep for food source.

Subterranean termites can remain hidden for a long time and you will not know they are there. These are the ones that will cause the most damage to your home. They live underground and tunnel the wood of your home. Termites have the ability to cover their tracks, leaving them hidden for until the damage is already done. Termite control costs can be staggering when this happens.

Termite Life Cycle:

Exterminators know the best way to find the correct termite control chemicals for an infestation is to understand the termite life cycle. This is because the way that the termite lives and breeds has a lot to do with eliminating the colony as a whole.

With most termite colonies, there will be the queen (and in some cases several queens) and the king. In most cases, these termites are the only ones that reproduce, but that is not always the case. The other termites will care for the queen and king termite's needs including feeding them around the clock.

The king and queen, if sheltered and cared for properly can live up to 25 years, although that is not the norm. A queen that is mature can lay thousands of eggs every year. Termite eggs have a two week incubation time and during that time, the worker termites will care for the eggs very carefully.

Nymph:

Once an egg hatches, it is called a nymph. The worker termites that are designated for caring for these young termites will feed the nymphs for two weeks. Their diet will consist of regurgitated food. During this two week period, the nymph will start changing and will molt. They will then become a part of the class of the colony as a soldier, worker, reproductive or supplementary reproductive.

If a nymph is to grow into a reproductive member of the colony, it will begin to grow and develop reproductive organs during this time. These termites will turn black and will gain sight. The wings will grow longer than its body.

Worker:

If the nymph is to grow into a worker, it will

not have reproductive organs and will not have eyes. These workers are blind and very fragile. Eventually, these worker termites will leave the colony and find food sources for the colony, usually feeding off of wood from buildings and other wood sources. The worker are vital to the survival of the colony and they represent the largest population in the colony. They will work around the clock to find food sources, feed others in the colony and building and repair the colony as needed.

Soldier:

If the termite grows into a soldier termite, it will develop into a long, armored bodied-insect. It will develop large pinchers, or jaws during the last molting. It will go to work defending the colony against ants and other enemies.

Reproductives:

If the termite develops into a reproductive member of the colony, it will leave the colony along with the others during the spring. Many of these swarmers do not survive. Some of them will and when they fall to the ground and shed their wings.

During this time, they are very vulnerable. They are often eaten by other insects and by birds. The males that make it through the swarm will find a mate and they will tunnel underground and start an underground nest. These are often the ones that will cause problems with your home. They will find food source (the wood of your home) and begin chewing away and building tunnels in the wood. This can sometimes be difficult to detect until a lot of damage is already done.

Some swarming termites will make it through and will start a new large colony. They will begin to reproduce and will produce workers and soldiers that will begin building a new colony for the king and queen. Because worker termites can only survive at a high humidity, they will move their colony to find the best temperature and moisture for survival.

The food that they are most attracted to are fungus infested wood, but if they cannot find it, they will feed off of new wood, too. The workers will secrete food material from their bodies and feed the reproductives and the soldiers.

TYPES OF TERMITES

There are several different species of termites. If you notice or suspect problems with termites in your home, the first step in finding an appropriate termite control baiting system or even home remedies for termite control is to determine what type of termites you are dealing with. This works because different species of termites will live and feed differently. In addition, there are many different species of termites that live all over the world.

In North American, there are four species of termites that are most commonly seen. These species include the formosan termite, the subterranean termite, the drywood termite and the dampwood termite. Each of these four types will live, feed and breed differently, so if you are facing a termite infestation, it is important to try to identify the type of termite that you have.

- *Formosan termite:*

This type of termite lives off of cellulose, or wood and wood substances. These are common invaders of homes in North America, but not as common as the other varieties. These are most common throughout the southern portions of the United States.

Formosan termites live underground levels, but unlike subterranean termites, they are more aggressive. They do not just live on dead wood, they also seek out living trees, which is different than most other species of termites. This species of termites originated from southern portions of China and were brought into North America during World War II.

Most common in Texas, these termites were first discovered in Pasadena in 1956. They have since spread across Texas and are commonly found termites in about 30 different Texas counties. They most often swarm between April and July and can cause more damage than any other type of termite found in North America.

While it takes a few years for a colony to reach its peak, an average Formosan colony can house thousands of damage-causing insects and can hollow wood so thin that it resembles a sheet of paper.

Formosan termites do prefer cellulose as their food source, but have been known to also attack other types of material including plastic, asphalt, plaster, copper and even lead.

These termites have the same caste structure as any other type of termite colony that includes the queen (or queens), the king, the workers, soldiers and the reproductives and secondary reproductives.

- *Subterranean termites:*

Subterranean termites get their name from where they live. They live below the ground. Many people mistakenly believe that all termites live in wood. This is not the case. Most subterranean termites live underground and come out to locate a food source. This species of termites normally live near the wooden food source of building structures and other dead wood. They tunnel up through the ground and get their food to take back into the colony.

Subterranean termites are normally the ones that cause the most damage to homes. In fact, it is estimated that these termites are the cause of approximately ninety percent of damage done to homes. In the United States alone, subterranean termites can cause up to three billion dollars worth of damage.

The bad news is that these termites are normally harder to treat than any other species of termites, even though they are the most common. These termites have the advantage of living underground and this makes locating and eradicating the colonies much more difficult than exterminating colonies that live in easy to find nests.

This species of termites mostly feed off of converted wood fiver and cellulose. They will eat the wood from the inside out making it hard to detect until a lot of damage has been done. These termites are normally found in warm tropical climates and hot arid climates, so they are common in the Southern parts of the United States.

Sometimes these termites are hard to detect. If you have an infestation of these termites around your home, there will be signs. The first sign that you have termites will be "swarmers". These are winged termites that are coming out of the tunnels to nest. It is not uncommon to see swarmers in the late summer and in the spring. When they drop their wings, you will see the wings on windowsills and in cobwebs.

Mud tunnels in your yard is another indication that that you have subterranean termites. These are often found on foundation walls and around the slabs of your home. If you find mud tunnels on your home, you can break them open to see if there are termites that are living.

If you suspect you have these termites around your home, you can also look for wood damage. Damaged wood is a good indication that you either have termites now or it has been infested in the past. Termite tunnels often follow the grain of the wood and may also have a spotted appearance. If you see signs such as these, then it is time that you call an exterminator.

- *Drywood termites:*

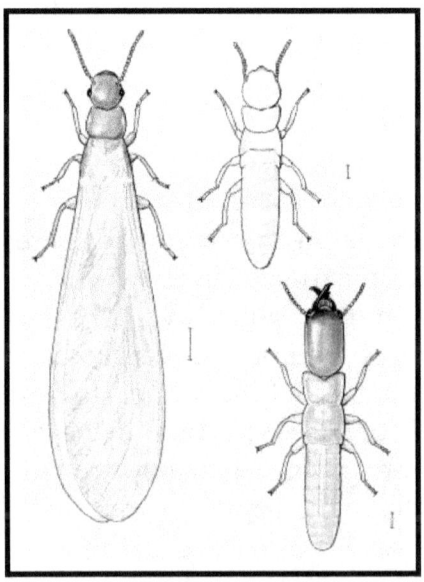

Another type of termite that is typically found in the United States is the drywood termite. These termites live about ground level and are very common, although not as damaging as other species. The interesting thing about these termites is that it often takes up to two years for signs to show that these termites have invaded. By then, a lot of damage is already done. You can often find drywood termites feeding off of dead wood and other similar food sources.

You will most commonly see drywood termites living and feeding off of undecayed wood that does not contain a lot of moisture. These termites do not need the soil to survive and live so these often cause damage to things like firewood, wooden furniture and other wooden pieces. Drywood termites are most commonly found in Virginia, Southern Florida and along the Gulf of Mexico.

DETECTING TERMITES

No one wants to deal with the problems and headaches that are associated with any species of termites. These causing-problem insects can quickly destroy a home and other wooden objects. In many cases, you may not even know that an infestation is occurring until the damage is done. There are ways that you can detect termites and early detection can mean the difference between expensive problems later down the road. Many people think that detecting termites is very hard and that only a professional exterminator can do the job. You can, however, learn signs to look for when you suspect a termite problem on your property.

Here are ways that a termite infestation is commonly caught:

- Termites are often accidently discovered when a homeowner is doing things in and around the home. If you drop something on the wood in your home and it dents, or if you accidently bump into the baseboards around your floors and it dents every easily, then that often means that the wood has weakened and termites are to blame.

  If you notice a large swarm of termites in your home or around your property, then chances are that you are facing an infestation and will need to call someone to inspect your home and surrounding area.

  Another way to tell if you are being attacked

by a termite infestation is if you see odd mud tracks in and around your home. These are often caused by the tunneling of subterranean termites and this means they have invaded the wood of your home. This mud is often found around the plasterwork and baseboards inside a home and around the foundation on the outside of a home.

If you have an exhaust fan that suddenly will not turn off or on, then you might have termites.

Termites will also cause the wood around your windows to take on a molted appearance through the varnish and will also cause odd looking bubbles through painted walls and trim.

- Termites are also often discovered when other work is being done to the home. If you are having work done to your home and they tell you they have seen signs of termites, then it is time to call an exterminator. They often show up when plumbing, painting and electrical work is being done.

- A home inspection will also turn up these pesky insects. If you look under your floors and see mud shelter tubes, then this is a tale-tell sign that you are experiencing termites.

You will also find termites if you look near wet areas of your home and find unusual uneven surfaces or bubbled areas.

If you are in your attic and the wood seems springy or hollow, then chances are you are dealing with termites.

Termites will drop their wings when they swarm. You can find these near an opening in a termite nest or shelter and in your home or in your yard. A large number of wings will indicate termites are nearby. These are most commonly found in the late fall and in the spring, so be aware and look for these signs.

- Professional detection:

    Professionals have some very advanced ways of zeroing in on termites without damaging your home. They will look for all of these signs mentioned above, but if they still haven't found them, they can employ other techniques.

    Some professional exterminators will encourage homeowners to have their home inspected twice a year for termites, even if there have been no problems. They will be able to tell right away if there is a problem.

    Professionals can use x-ray techniques to tell whether or not a structure has been infested. They can scan the wall with a special tool and see any infestation or sign of past problems on a monitor. This is quite effective when termites are likely to hide in small and hard to reach places, albeit quite expensive.

Ultrasound techniques are also used for detecting termites. This technique uses a special headset and microphone to "hear" the termites.

- Other signs of termites include:

    Wood damage

    Fecal droppings

    Visible nests or mounds

    Holes in the yard

NATURAL TERMITE CONTROL

When you first see signs of termites, then you should take it seriously. It is always better to call a professional, rather than trying at home methods. However, some people will tell you that they have had some success in natural termite control, which will be looked at in depth.

Getting rid of a termite problem is not like getting rid of flies or ants. With those types of pest, you can use some bait or spray and pretty much get rid of the problem. With termites, extermination can be quite a bit more complicated and expensive. Next, we will take a look at various termites exterminating and control methods.

Natural Termite Control and Extermination:

First on the list, are the many natural and organic ways that you can use to eliminate termites from your home. While many professional do not recommend that you try and get rid of the termites yourself, many homeowners have reported great success with these methods.

In addition to being cheaper on the pocketbook, some homeowners like the idea of using organic termite control and natural termite control methods because they are safer for the environment.

Since the forties, the way to get rid of termites is to spray the ground around the structure with chlorinated hydrocarbons, which is a very potent and dangerous chemical. When sprayed on the foundation and on the soil around the home, it can cause damage to the area.

These chemicals are very effective on killing termites, but they have also been known to cause a wide variety of health issues. In fact, they can poison the water and cause problems with people who suffer from upper respiratory problems.

So, what kind of good-for-you termite control methods can you use? What works and what does not? There are several proven methods that will help you get rid of the termites in and around your home. If you are concerned about the health of those in your home or you are concerned with the environment, here is a look of some of the methods that you can check into if you are afraid of using chemicals.

- *Biological Control:*

    Believe it or not, you can use biological control when you are combating a termite problem. There are many different types of these controls that are being used with some success. One employs the use of parasite organisms called nematodes.

    Nematodes are very small worm-like creatures that will take over termites. They will crawl into the termite body openings and release bacteria that will kill the termites.

    This method will usually work within a

matter of days. While that is great news for the homeowner, this method is still being experimented with on a large scale. It can work very well for a small termite population, but it will not work as well for a large termite problem.

If you are interested in using nematodes, one method that might work well is to use them alongside of some other form of natural termite control.

There are websites that sell nematodes and other organic termite control products. You can buy nematodes in vials. One vial will work in 40 gallons of water and can treat about 40 feet of foundation. Nematodes can be applied directly to affected areas, nests and colonies or poured into tubes interested near an infestation.

The result will be that the nematodes will attack the termites and will eventually kill off the queen and other reproductives in the colony, resulting in the colony to die off.

- *Orange oil termite control:*

  Another very popular method of organic and natural remedy for termite control is the use of orange oil. Citrus oil termite control is quite effective at killing off termites because orange oil is a natural insecticide for many types of pests, especially for termites.

Orange oil is extracted from the peels of oranges and contains an ingredient called d-limonene, which is the natural insecticide. While this natural chemical is toxic to insects, it does not harm people, pets or the environment.

You may even find some professional exterminators that specialize in natural termite control products/services, including the use of orange oil termite control.

Companies that use natural home remedies for termite control know that many people are concerned about using toxic chemicals around the home. They will use the orange oil and inject it near the problem areas.

This is a great alternative to fumigation and does not require you to have to leave your home overnight after treatment, which is a plus, especially if you are comparing tenting versus orange oil for termite control.

Orange oil can be purchased on the Internet and through suppliers of organic and natural pest products. You can buy orange oil that can be diluted with water, or in full strength.

- *Sodium Borate:*

Another natural method for exterminating termites is called sodium borate. This is a very popular method for a more natural approach at killing off termites.

It is so effective that it will actually prevent termites, so some home builders will use sodium borate foam or a type of dust treatment in and around where they are building and on the wood used to build a house to prevent future problems. Some homebuilders will also inject the substance directly into wood that is being used to build a home. Homeowners that know this is useful will often request this type of treatment during a home build.

While sodium borate has proven effect measures to prevent termites while a home is being built, it may not be so effective at killing off an infestation after a home is completed. It is hard to kill off a large infestation of termites with sodium borate.

Sodium borate began to gain favor in the early 90s and is now marketed under a variety of names including Tim-Bor, Nibor-D, Bora-Care and Jecta Gel.

How do borate treatments work to kill off termites? When injected into a problem area, sodium borate will kill off termites by starving them to death. They won't die off immediately, but will in a matter of a couple of days.

When ingested, the sodium borate will attack and kill the tiny protozoa that line the termite's intestinal tract. The protozoa are what make the digestion of wood possible and without them; the termites will starve and die.It is fairly easy to apply sodium borate. You will simply follow the directions on the package that you buy. In most cases, you will mix a certain amount of the product along with a gallon of water and spray it on the wood.

It can also be applied with a paintbrush. If you saturate the wood properly, it can provide your home with several years of protection, which is great insurance for your home. This is one of the many great pre construction termite methods.

Before you decide which method you want to try to get rid of termites, you might want to take the time to do some research and find out which option will work best for you. Many of these natural remedies are cheaper than calling a professional, but you must also keep in mind that if you do not kill off all of the termites, then you could face costly repairs to your home later down the line. Only a professional can inspect and tell if all of the termites are gone.

OTHER FORMS OF
TERMITE CONTROL

There are many methods of killing termites and there are just as many ways that you can prevent them. When you think you have termites, you may be tempted to go to the local home improvement store and look through the available ant and termite control products. Many of these products that are on the shelf will work to a degree.

In order to make sure that you have taken care of all of the termites when you have an infestation, it is always recommended that you call a professional. Professional termite exterminators have many means in which to detect and kill off termite colonies so that your problem goes away quickly. The following are all great home and apt pest and termite control methods that professionals will use.

- *Insecticides:*

    There are many insecticides that are very effective and useful in the treatment of termites. If you call an exterminator, some form of insecticide will be used. Some of these chemicals are much stronger than others and some are more hazardous than others. A professional exterminator will be able to recommend the proper treatment depending on the type of infestation your building structure has. For example, insecticide for dry wood termites will have specific dry wood termite control in the home. If you have another species of termites, something else will be recommended.

Termiticides, or in other words, chemicals use to kill and treat termites will be applied to the outbreak to prevent future infestations. Continuous barriers are important in the successful treatment of termites. When using an insecticide for termite control, you will want to make sure that you are getting a continuous chemical barrier not only on the termite mound or nest, but also in the surrounding soil, as termites can tunnel a long way. You must also make sure that you are treating the foundation of the building structure and that any other infected area is treated in the same way.

If you go to the store and decide to buy insecticide treatments and try and kill the infestation on your own, you have to remember that one treatment will not do the trick. Placing only one treatment will encourage reinfestation in no time at all.

There are many different types of insecticides that are available over the counter and through your exterminator. In order to find the one that is right for the job, you have to first determine the type of termites that you have and then find out how large of an infestation you are talking about.

Liquid insecticide, also called termiticide, is often applied on the soil. These have been used for decades, but the ones that have been developed recently work at killing the termite and not just repelling them as it used to work.

Some of the newer insecticides works as a non-repellant. This means that they work to kill the termites that tunnel into the treatment. These non-repellents are very reliable and often work the first time.

If you decide to buy insecticide to kill off the termites, then do your research. There are many different products on the market. You can buy undiluted sprays, diluted sprays, foams and other varieties. These are quite pricey, but they often work well.

Some popular brands include:

- Bifen IT
- Bora Care
- Dominion
- Borrada D
- Borrada LP
- Cyper TC
- Demon TC
- Talstar One
- Tim-bor
- Permethrins
- Phantom
- Premise
- Talstar P

Termite Baits:

Next up are termite baits. Termite baits are quite easy to use and effective. They are also cost-effective if you are not facing a bad infestation. If you are interested in using termite baits, it is recommended that you call and exterminator before using. They can tell you whether or not a termite bait will work for you.

Termite baiting is considered a form of broad termite treatment. They usually are made up of cardboard, paper or other type of food that termites like to eat along with a lethal chemical that will kill the termite. All termite baits are strategically placed below the ground in plastic stations. If you have a problem with termites indoors, you can find baits that can be placed inside the house near active mud tunnels.

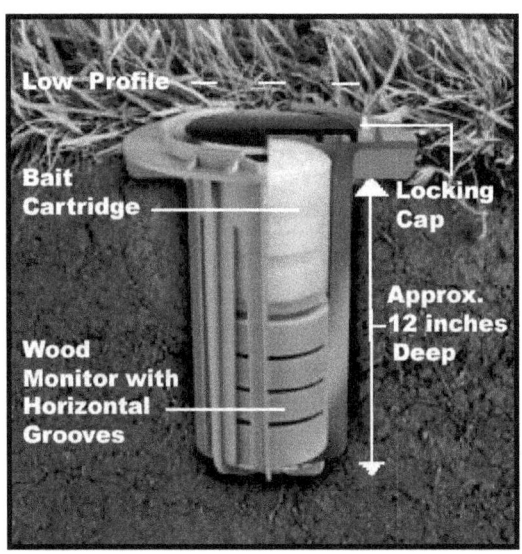

- How do these baits work?

    The worker termites are attracted to the food that is placed into the baits. They eat the food and carry it back to the other termites in the colony. The chemical that is mixed with the food will eventually start killing off the termites in the colony. When the termite population begins to die, the colony dies off.

    Termite baits are often used along with chemicals to ensure that the termites die and do not return. These are especially useful in areas where termites are visible.

- Challenges of using baits:

    There are challenges in using termite baits. When worker termites begin exploring the area for food, they do not see or smell. Baits must be placed where the termites will discover them. For this reason, one or two baits will not do the job very efficiently.

- Placing the baits

    If you decide to place baits in your yard, it is recommended that you place them at fixed intervals ten to twenty feet apart in your yard. You should especially concentrate on areas where there are known termites. Also keep in mind that termites are attracted to moisture and dead wood. Place your yard baits around any wood piles, moist areas and tree stumps.

- How fast baits work:

  Also keep in mind that when you use termite baits, they will not work the same way that insecticide works. Insecticide is designed to kill on contact.

  Termite baits work over a period of time. While you can never guarantee how fast the baits will work, most will start to work within a few days. You have to allow time for these baits to become effective. How fast these work will also depend on the time of year, whether or not it is time for swarmers and the temperature and moisture in the area. If the conditions for the termites are ideal, it will be easy to see the baits working faster. If it is not ideal, the baits will take longer to work. Placing baits during the cold weather will also lend itself to slower than average results.

- Using above ground baits

  Above ground baits are also very effective for some people trying to get of termites on their property. These work best when they are installed in the path of known and active termites and work very well when a mud tube has been broken. They are also useful in baiting termites on and near infested wood and drywall.

  In fact, if you are looking at using above ground baits, you might be interested to know that they often work faster than in ground termite baits. Sometimes homeowners decided to use both in ground and above ground baits for the maximum effectiveness.

- Using baits:

Whether you are using in ground or above ground baits to help with your termite problem, there are ways that they need to be monitored and cared for so that you get the best results. This is true for using baits that are professionally installed or using baits that you install yourself.

After the baits have been installed, they will have to be carefully monitored. Each station that is installed will be set with some amount of termite food. If this food is attacked, then you know that termites have found the bait.

After they have been installed, you will check for bait delivery. When the termites are found near or in the station, the untreated wood will then be replaced with food that contains a lethal chemical. Sometimes a slow acting growth inhibitor is used.

The termites will take the bait and their pheromone scented trail will led other termites to the baited area. The result is that the termites will start to feed off the affected bait and start to die off.

If you find that a bait is being "hit" it is often very effective to add more baits to the same area to increase the effectiveness.

There are many termite baiting systems on the market. These can be installed by a professional termite exterminator, or you can try your hand at some of the over the counter varieties.

Some of the more popular brands include:

- ◊ Firstline
- ◊ Exterra
- ◊ Subterfuge
- ◊ Advance Termite Bait System
- ◊ Spectracide Terminate

These bait systems are quite comparable to each other and all work in about the same way. You can buy almost all of these termite baiting systems at your local home improvement store for about $100, for a basic kit. If your property is very large or you are facing a large termite problem, then the price of your baiting system can go up. This will depend on how many baiting stations you will need to use.

That price will sound very good to homeowners that have gotten an estimate from a professional. If you call an exterminator out to place baiting systems on your property, you can easily expect to pay at least $1000.

As with any termite problem and treatment system, you have to do your research and know what you are doing if you plan on tackling the problem on your own. If you intend on using baiting as a way to get rid of termites, you have to keep in mind that it will not work at all unless you use proper methods. You must make sure that you have installed the stations correctly and adequately and that they are properly monitored and maintained. Ongoing bait replenishing is also a must for baiting to work properly.

Tenting:

In the world of termite extermination, you might hear a lot about what is called "tenting". Tenting is a technique used for homes and other buildings that have a very large termite infestation. When traditional methods won't work, tenting is a way to treat a large structure at once.

If you have a large number of termites in your home and you call a professional, the company may recommend this method. This is normally reserved for infestations that affect an entire structure — when the majority of the home has been infested. The termite company will come out to your home and encase your entire home and property with a tent. They will then release very strong termite insecticide to being the killing process.

Here are some frequently asked questions about this form of termite extermination:

- What are the pros of tenting for a termite infestation?

  Tenting a home for a termite infestation is sometimes the only way that the process will work if there is a large infestation. The entire area will be sealed off and the gas that is used will immediately kill all of the termites, including the queen and the king. This is often the fastest and most effective way to make sure that every termite has been killed and that you are on your way to a termite free home.

- What are the disadvantages of using this method for killing the termites?

  Tenting is often not the preferred method of termite extermination. There are several reasons for this. First of all, it is extremely expensive. It could cost more than $3000 for an average sized home. It is also very dangerous. The chemicals that are used are highly toxic and when a home is tented, warning signs are put up all over the place. In addition, when a home is tented, the homeowners must leave the home for several days. When they return, everything must be cleaned out. Tenting also only works properly for drywood termites, so the type of termites that you have will determine whether nor not tenting will work for you.

- How is a home prepared for termite tenting extermination?

  If you are going the tenting route for your infestation of termites, there are several steps that will be taken to ensure the safety of everyone in the home and those around your home.

  First of all, you will have to pack up many of the things in your home. Food must be removed or sealed in special plastic bags. Many homeowners also choose to remove clothing and bedding from the home or have these items sealed in plastic. If you have any pets, they will also have to be removed from the premises. Plants will need to be removed as well. Outside plants and shrubs that are very close to the perimeter of the home may need to be removed so that the company can get closer to the foundation to work. Anything of the top of the house such as antenna, chiminey caps and weather vanes will have to be removed before the home is tented.

  After the initial preparation, the homeowners (and pets) will have to stay away from the home for up to two days, if not longer. During this time, the termite company will cover the home with a tent. This tent will be placed so that it is secure and tight around the property. Warning signs will be posted to keep other people away from the area while the treatment is in process.

When the tenting is complete, the fumigation process will begin. The gas will be released into the home and will be allowed to circulate for at least 24 hours.

Usually, during the second day, after the fumigation is complete, the tent around your home will be removed. The insecticide will be aired out. The following day, the company will check to make sure that no gas remains in the home and that the termites are dead. They will use special equipment to gauge the gas levels in the house. You will not be allowed back into your home until the levels are safe. When it is safe for you to re-enter, you will be given cleaning instructions.

- Is tenting safe?

When the gas is released into your home, it is toxic and for that reason, you are asked to leave the area for a couple of days. However, once the gas has cleared, it is safe for you to return to your home. Most professionals use chemicals that do not adhere to surfaces so you do not have to worry about a residue, although most homeowners do want to clean out their home upon returning.

- Does tenting get rid of all of the termites that are in the home?

Tenting is designed to kill off all living

termites, however, you will be told that it will not kill the eggs. The good news is that even though these eggs will hatch, they will quickly die since there will be no worker termites to feed and care for them. This process will not be effective for subterranean termites, so it is always a good idea to have your property treated for these types of termites as well.

You should also be aware that while this is a very effective means of killing off termites, there is no guarantee that they will never return. Only prevention methods can help make sure that you do not get a re-infestation.

PREVENTING TERMITES

If you have fought a termite infestation in your home and you are now free and clear of these little pests, you might want to know what you can do to prevent them from causing problems in the future. Even if you have never had a problem with termites, it is a great idea to know how you can keep them away from your home.

Termites do not just show up. They are attracted to your home because it is an ideal living condition for them. There is the right amount of food, moisture and shelter. When you want to prevent termites, you can make sure that you make your home less pleasing to them.

Here are some things that you can do to keep the termites away from your home and your property.

- *Avoid moisture build up around your home, especially around the foundation:*

    Make sure that you divert the flow of water away from your home by using downspouts, splash blocks and gutters. You can also slope the soil around your foundation so that water flows away from your home.

- *Check the humidity:*

    Termites like the humidity. You can reduce the chances of a termite infestation by reducing the humidity in hard to reach places just as your attic and crawl spaces of your home and around your property.

- *Get rid of wood scraps:*

  As you know, termites eat wood. If you are building a home or other new construction on your property, gather up those small pieces of scrap wood and haul them away. Avoid burying any scraps of wood.

- *Remove dead wood:*

  If you have an old tree stump or other dead wood on your property, especially if it is very close to your home, make sure you remove it to prevent termites.

- *Never stack firewood too close to your home:*

  Avoid the temptation to stack firewood too close to the foundation of your home and near other building structures. Never store wood in crawl spaces.

- *Avoid wooden trellises and vines:*

  If you live in an area that is prone to termite infestations, avoid using wooden trellis against your home. Vines can also cause problems and will attract termites.

- *Reinforce the foundation:*

If you are building, make sure that your foundation is reinforced to prevent cracking. Cracked foundations are very inviting to termites.

- *Consider pre-treatment on a new building structure:*

    You can used borates on new wood while a structure is being built. This will discourage termites for many years when it is used properly. In fact, many home builders will use this form of termite prevention if you ask. You can also prevent termites by using pre-treated wood.

- *Avoid wood contact with the soil around your home:*

    Many homeowners can prevent attracting termites by simply making sure that wood does not come in contact with the soil on a property.

- *Avoid wood mulch:*

    Wood mulch and wood chips are very popular among landscapers and gardeners. However, they are also a feeding ground for termites. There are many great alternatives to wood mulch that can be used around the home including pea gravel, recycled products and crushed stone. These will not attract termites as wood mulch will over time.

- *Have annual inspections:*

    A simple annual home inspection in and around your home can easily detect the presence of termites before it is too late. Keep records and take special notes of any insect damage. If you see damage, make sure that you take action right away and don't wait until it is too late or until further damage is done to your home. Many exterminators will actually help you with annual inspections for a small fee—and they know just what to look for when dealing with termites and other damaging insects.

- *Know what to look for:*

    A key in preventing termites is to know what you are looking for. Know the type of termites that are common in your area and what they are most attracted to. Learn the signs of these termites and make sure you know what mud tunnels and termite dirt piles look like so that you know what to look for upon your annual inspection.

- *Control moisture in crawl spaces:*

    You can control moisture (that is very attractive to termites) in small crawl spaces by laying films of polyethylene in these areas under the foundation.

- *Maintain adequate ventilation:*

  This means in your crawl spaces, attic and through foundation wall vents.

- *Prune the plants:*

  You can help prevent termites by making sure that you prune back plants that sit close to your home on a regular basis. This will not only help keep wood away from your home, but it will also help decrease the amount of moisture and mold that will build up against wooden walls of your home.

- *Check your sprinklers:*

  Sprinklers that are left to hit the wooden parts of your home invites a build-up of moisture and this will invite those pesky termites to nest and fed off of your home. Make sure that the sprinklers are not keeping your fence and the sides of your home wet when they run.

- *Seal wood:*

  If you are using wood around your home, such as a wood deck, shutters and other trims, make sure they are appropriately sealed, especially around the edges where it meets the wall.

- *Use sand:*

  Termites do not like sand, so if you are

concerned about termites, you can use a sand barrier under wood fence posts, wooden decks and other wood structures that are on your property.

- *Fill all cracks:*

    Annual home inspections are important. If you are inspecting your home, you may find cracks in the concrete or other areas of your home. These cracks are very inviting to termites, so do not let them go. Make sure that you fill these cracks right away. If you live in an area that is prone to earthquakes, you should fill any and all cracks with sealer as soon as the house settles.

When you know what to look for when are inspecting your home, you will go a long way in preventing termites from attacking your home. Make sure that you keep these tips in mind.

CHOOSING AN EXTERMINATOR

Once you have discovered that you have an infestation of termites, you may feel panicked. There are many people that think that your house will be ruined and it can never be sold to another buyer after termites. While it is true that extensive termite damage can decrease the value of your home, your home is not necessarily ruined. There are ways you can tackle the problem.

One of the best ways to deal with termites is to get a licensed professional to help you. There are many trained exterminators out there and all they do is deal with termites. If you have termites, it is very important that you find a reputable company that can walk you through the process of getting rid of the termites and can help you prevent them in the future.

Finding a good termite professional means that you must find one that is up to date on all the latest knowledge and technology and has all the newest equipment to help located and eradicate the termite colonies on your property.

No matter where you live, you can start finding help by looking up termite professionals in your area in your phonebook or by using an Internet search engine. You can try key words that include the word "termite" and your location (such as "termite control in los angeles", "texas termite control" and "termite control florida"). If you already know of a company you want to use, you can check to see if that company has good ratings and reviews by other companies. Simply get online and use a search engine. Type in the name of the company and the location (such as "arrow termite control Atlanta g"). You will be able to find any ratings and reviews that will help you make your choice. You will also want to make sure that the company you are using is license to treat termites in your area. You can do the same with a search engine. (Just try something like, "florida termite control license".)

It is important that when you are dealing with a termite problem that you find a good company that is honest and trustworthy. You want to make sure that you are getting the best results for the money that you will spend.

Here are some more tips that will help you locate and find apt pest and termite control companies.

- *Stay calm:*

    As soon as some homeowners hear the words "termite infestation", they panic. They are likely to hire the first exterminator they call without checking for license or credentials. This is not recommended. You need to stay calm and make sure that you are choosing a company wisely. Don't settle for the first one. You will end up regretting your decision later and may end up paying a lot more money unless you shop around.

- *Shop around:*

    Nothing says that you have to pick the first company you call. Some termite companies know that homeowners get desperate when dealing with termites. These are the same companies that will try to rush you into a contract. This is the time when you need to slow down and shop around. Even if it takes you several days to choose a company to use, it will not make much of a difference. Do your research, take your time and choose wisely.

- *Know what you are dealing with before you call anyone*:

    Before you call an exterminator out to your home, you need to make sure you know what you are dealing with. If you have someone come out to look at your home, an inspection will cost you. If you are on a tight budget, learn how to look for termites and if you find signs of them, then call someone out. Most companies can come out and give you a basic inspection and an estimate without locking you into any contract.

- *Get recommendations:*

    If termites are a problem in your area, then chances are there is someone you know that has had to hire an exterminator in the past. This is a great time to call your friends and neighbors to get recommendations. You can also get online, as mentioned early, and research the various companies that service your area.

- *Get a proper inspection:*

A proper termite inspection is more than just having a company out to tell you that you do have termites. A good company will do a complete and thorough inspection in and around your home. They will take notes and look for damage. They will be able to tell you if there are signs of past termites or if you have active termites.

- *Get an estimate:*

After the initial inspection, you should expect an estimate for the treatment of your home. An estimate should include the type of recommended treatments, how many treatments should be expected to treat the problem, warranties, and any guarantees. You should also make sure that the estimate you are getting is a firm price or a "ball park" figure before you proceed.

- *Know your options and ask questions:*

When you get your estimate, it is important that you understand what is included in your treatment. You have a lot of treatment options and a professional company can help you understand each one and which one is right for your home. You also do not want to be taken advantage of during and after your treatment, so take the time to clarify anything that you do not understand and ask questions before having the work done.

- *Understand the treatment process:*

    Once you choose a professional, make sure you know the differences between the treatment options. You can have soil and sand barriers put into place, baits placed around the perimeter of your home, fumigation and even tenting. In some cases, the company may recommend a variety of treatments that are used together for the maximum results. They may also offer some alternative options if that is right for your home. There are many treatment options and you need ot take the time to make sure you know which one is right before hiring anyone.

- *Getting more than one quote:*

    If you get more than one quote for the treatment of your home, you should tell the companies you are working with. That is a professional courtesy and you may find that the company you want to deal with over another might offer you a better deal if you have gotten a lower estimate from another company.

CONCLUSION

No one wants to deal with the problems cause by termites. Even a small infestation can cause a lot of damage to the home and property. No matter how big or small your termite problem is, you will find that as a homeowner, it is important to deal with the situation as soon as you possibly can so that you do not end up with even bigger and more expensive problems in the near future.

You now know that termites can ruin a home and termites do not care if you live in a small apartment in a big city or if you live in a huge house out on the golf course. If the conditions around your home are ideal, the termites will be attracted to the moisture, shelter and food that your home provides to them. Once the queen has nested, she will begin building the population in her colony and will live and breed for a long time to come on your home.

When a termite colony makes its way into your home, you can expect a lot of damage. There are signs you can watch for when it comes to termites. Most people will first notice termites as they swarm in the spring and the late fall. Even if you don't see the termites swarming and looking for shelter, you will be able to see their wings as they shed them. You can also know that you have a termite problem if you notice a visible nest on your property or find mud tubes or tunnels on or around the foundation of your home.

Termites are costly and once you know that you have them, you need to make sure that you deal with them right away. You should not wait to call someone out to help you get rid of the infestation. Waiting can cause further damage to your home.

The good news is that there are many products available that will help you take care of the problem before it is too late.

www.ingramcontent.com/pod-product-compliance
Lightning Source LLC
LaVergne TN
LVHW051849080426
835512LV00018B/3166